The Cost of Ignoring Change Management

How Neglecting Change Management Derails Digital Transformation

PALLAVI NIGAM

Preface

The Hidden Reason Digital Transformations Fail

When I first started working on **technology transformation projects**, I was convinced that success was all about **choosing the right technology**. If companies invested in **AI-powered analytics, cloud computing, and automation tools**, they'd naturally become **more efficient, innovative, and competitive**.

I was wrong.

After two decades of working across industries like **FMCG, pharma, construction, and real estate**, I've seen firsthand how companies spend **millions** on digital transformation—only to end up with systems that **nobody uses, employees resent, and leaders quietly regret.**

The common denominator?

Neglecting change management.

It turns out that **people—not technology—are the real challenge** in digital transformation.

- Employees who **refuse to adopt new systems** because they weren't involved in the decision-making process.
- Leadership teams that assume **buying software equals success**—without preparing for cultural shifts.

- Organizations that believe **resistance to change is the problem**, when in reality, it's a **symptom of bad leadership and poor execution.**

This book exists because I got tired of watching **great technology fail** due to **poor change management**.

Why I Wrote This Book

I wrote this book for **leaders, managers, and transformation teams** who are frustrated by the disconnect between **digital vision and execution.**

But let's be clear—this is **not** a dry, corporate textbook filled with **consultant jargon and unrealistic frameworks**.

Instead, I've packed it with **real-world stories** of digital transformation failures (and successes) from **FMCG, pharma, construction, and real estate**.

Some of these stories are **painful**. Others are **hilarious**. But all of them reveal the **same hard truth**:

Technology alone doesn't drive change. People do.

And if you fail to bring your people along, your digital transformation will fail—no matter how advanced your tools are.

What You'll Learn in This Book

By the time you finish this book, you'll understand:

- **Why employees resist change—and how to turn them into champions instead.**
- **The biggest mistakes companies make when rolling out new digital systems.**

- **How to create a culture where digital adoption happens naturally (without force).**
- **Practical, no-nonsense strategies for making digital transformation stick.**

This book isn't about **hypothetical theories**—it's about **real, tested strategies** that work in the trenches of digital transformation.

A Final Thought Before You Start

If you're reading this book, chances are you're either:

1. About to start a **digital transformation journey** and want to get it right.
2. In the middle of one that's **going sideways**—and need to fix it before it becomes a disaster.

Either way, I want to assure you: **It's not too late.**

By **putting people at the center of digital transformation**, you can avoid costly failures and turn **resistance into momentum**.

And that's exactly what this book will show you how to do.

Many Thanks

Pallavi Nigam

TABLE OF CONTENTS

The Cost of Ignoring Change: How Neglecting Change Management Derails Digital Transformation

---

Part 1: Understanding the Digital Transformation and Change Management Nexus

1. Introduction: The Digital Transformation Paradox

- What digital transformation really means
- Why companies invest in technology but fail in execution
- The role of change management in successful transformation

2. The Psychology of Change: Why People Resist

- The human factor in digital transformation
- Psychological barriers to change
- The role of leadership in managing resistance

3. The True Cost of Ignoring Change Management

- Financial implications of failed transformations
- Impact on workforce morale and productivity
- Case studies of costly failures

Part 2: Industry Insights – When Digital Transformation Goes Wrong

4. FMCG: Automation Without Adoption

- Story: A multinational FMCG company implements an AI-driven supply chain system, but employees resist due to lack of training and engagement.
- Lessons learned: Why front-line employees must be part of the transformation journey.

5. Construction: The Digital Blueprint That Never Took Off

- Story: A construction firm invests in Building Information Modeling (BIM), but site engineers revert to traditional methods.
- Lessons learned: How digital tools fail without workforce buy-in.

6. Pharma: Compliance and Chaos

- Story: A pharmaceutical company shifts to a new regulatory compliance system, leading to confusion and missed deadlines.
- Lessons learned: Why stakeholder engagement is critical in highly regulated industries.

7. Real Estate: Smart Systems, Stubborn Mindsets

- Story: A real estate giant introduces a digital property management system, but property managers resist change.
- Lessons learned: The need for cultural transformation alongside technological adoption.

Part 3: Winning Strategies for Successful Digital Transformation

8. Change Management Frameworks That Work

- Overview of Kotter's Change Model, ADKAR, and other frameworks
- How to integrate change management with digital strategies

9. Leadership's Role in Digital Success

- How leaders can drive transformation effectively
- Case studies of successful leadership-driven change

10. Building a Change-Ready Culture

- Creating a culture that embraces digital evolution
- Encouraging continuous learning and adaptability

11. The Roadmap to Digital Success

- Practical steps to ensure successful digital transformation
- The role of ongoing training, feedback, and agile adaptation

---

Conclusion: The Future of Change Management in Digital Transformation

- Emerging trends in change management
- The next wave of digital transformation challenges
- Final thoughts on ensuring sustainable digital success

Chapter 1: The Digital Transformation Paradox

Why Technology Alone Won't Save You

The Digital Dream vs. Reality

We live in an era where "digital transformation" is the corporate world's favorite buzzword. Companies throw around phrases like *AI-driven workflows*, *automation-first strategies*, and *cloud-native ecosystems*, hoping to impress shareholders and justify the millions—sometimes billions—spent on new technologies.

But let's be honest: most digital transformation initiatives **fail spectacularly**. According to research, more than **70% of digital transformation projects flop**, not because the technology is bad, but because the people using it **weren't ready, willing, or equipped to change**.

I've spent the last two decades working on technology transformation projects across industries, and if there's one universal truth I've learned, it's this: **You can install the most sophisticated software in the world, but if the people using it hate it, your project is doomed**.

You'd be amazed at how many organizations spend **millions on cutting-edge tech but pennies on helping their employees actually adopt it**. It's like buying a Formula 1 car for someone who has never driven before and then being shocked when they crash into the first wall they see.

Still not convinced? Let's look at two contrasting stories—one where digital transformation ended in disaster, and another where it led to extraordinary success.

Failure Story: The $100 Million Chocolate Meltdown at Hershey's

Picture this: it's Halloween season, the busiest time of the year for candy sales, and Hershey's, one of the biggest chocolate manufacturers in the world, has just invested **$100 million** in a brand-new Enterprise Resource Planning (ERP) system. The goal? To revolutionize their supply chain and increase efficiency.

Sounds like a smart move, right?

Well, here's what actually happened:

- Hershey's rushed the implementation, ignoring critical warnings from IT and supply chain experts.
- Employees weren't properly trained on the new system (because apparently, learning on the fly is a legitimate corporate strategy).
- The system went live **right before peak candy-buying season**, and—surprise, surprise—it didn't work.

The result? Hershey's **failed to deliver $150 million worth of orders**. That's right—shelves across the U.S. sat empty while desperate parents searched for last-minute Halloween candy. Even worse, Hershey's stock price **dropped 8% overnight**.

The lesson? **No matter how advanced a system is, if people don't know how to use it—or if the transition is rushed—the technology is useless.**

Success Story: Microsoft's Culture Overhaul Under Satya Nadella

Now, let's switch gears and talk about a transformation that actually worked.

Back in 2014, Microsoft was in trouble. The once-dominant tech giant was struggling to compete with the likes of Google and Apple. Internally, the company was plagued by **silos, bureaucracy, and a toxic "know-it-all" culture** that stifled innovation.

Enter **Satya Nadella**, the new CEO, who realized Microsoft's biggest problem wasn't technology—it was **people and culture**.

Instead of launching yet another expensive IT overhaul, Nadella focused on **changing mindsets**:

- He introduced a **growth mindset philosophy**, encouraging employees to experiment and learn.
- He **broke down internal silos**, fostering collaboration across teams.
- He shifted Microsoft's focus toward **cloud computing**, driving the company into new markets.

The results?

- Microsoft's **market value skyrocketed from $300 billion in 2014 to over $2 trillion by 2023**.
- The company became a leader in cloud computing and AI.
- Employee satisfaction and innovation levels soared.

The lesson? **Digital transformation isn't just about upgrading technology—it's about upgrading mindsets.**

The Invisible Roadblock: People Hate Change

So, why did Hershey's fail while Microsoft thrived? The answer is simple: **people resist change**.

If you've ever tried convincing your parents to stop writing down their passwords in a notebook, you know exactly what I mean.

Employees resist digital transformation for three main reasons:

1. **Fear of the Unknown** – "Will this AI replace my job?"
2. **Lack of Training and Support** – "I have no idea how to use this new system, but sure, let's pretend I do."
3. **Change Fatigue** – "First, we switched to an ERP. Then a CRM. Now we have AI bots handling emails? Just let me do my job!"

Most companies assume people will just "figure it out." Spoiler alert: **they won't**.

The High Cost of Ignoring Change Management

Hershey's isn't the only company that learned this lesson the hard way. Consider these additional cases of digital disaster:

- **Ford's $400 Million Digital Overhaul Failure (2019)** – Ford tried modernizing its software development processes but **ignored resistance from employees**, leading to a complete rollback of the initiative.
- **BBC's $150 Million Digital Media Failure** – The BBC spent years trying to develop a digital content management system but failed due to **poor leadership and disengaged employees**.
- **GE's IoT Platform Collapse** – General Electric launched a billion-dollar IoT platform called Predix, but due to **lack of clear leadership and employee buy-in**, the project crashed and burned.

And then there are companies like **Netflix, Amazon, and Tesla**, which have flourished because they understand one fundamental truth: **successful digital transformation is 80% about people and only 20% about technology**.

The Key Takeaway: People First, Tech Second

Here's the harsh reality: **Digital transformation isn't about technology. It's about people.**

I've spent **two decades** watching companies make the same mistake over and over—betting big on software, ignoring the human side, and then scratching their heads when things go south.

This book isn't going to teach you how to implement SAP or roll out AI-driven customer service bots. Instead, it will show you:

- **Real-life stories** from FMCG, construction, pharmaceuticals, and real estate, where companies either nailed or completely botched their digital transformation.
- **The psychology of change** and why people resist new technology.
- **Proven strategies** to get employees on board and make transformation stick.

Because at the end of the day, if your employees aren't ready for change, **no amount of AI, automation, or digital wizardry will save you.**

Chapter 2: The Psychology of Change – Why People Resist

Why Your Employees Would Rather Wrestle a Bear Than Learn a New System

---

Change is Hard (And That's an Understatement)

Let's face it: **people hate change**. Sure, we love the idea of progress—until it demands that we, you know, actually *change something*.

If you've ever tried to switch your parents from cable TV to Netflix, you've probably experienced the full force of human resistance.

- *"Where are the channels?"*
- *"Why do I have to type the name of the show?"*
- *"What do you mean, I can't just press '9' for my favorite channel?"*

Now, imagine introducing a **new AI-powered ERP system** to thousands of employees who've been using Excel spreadsheets since the early 2000s. It's not going to go well unless you have a strategy for handling that resistance.

I've spent **two decades working on technology transformation projects**, and I've seen everything—from employees sabotaging new systems out of spite to entire departments pretending the change never happened. And every time a company ignores the *human* side of change, the results are catastrophic.

Before we dive into *how* to fix this problem, let's first explore **why** people resist change.

Why People Resist Change: The Three Universal Fears

Most employees don't resist change because they're lazy or difficult. They resist because of three core fears:

1. The Fear of the Unknown – "Will this replace me?"

Let's talk about **PharmaCo**, a mid-sized pharmaceutical company that decided to implement a state-of-the-art AI-driven compliance tracking system. The system was supposed to streamline **FDA documentation** and **reduce manual errors**.

Great idea, right?

Except that the **regulatory affairs team**—whose entire job was handling compliance—thought this meant **they were about to be replaced by robots**.

So, what did they do?

- They **ignored** the new system.
- They **continued using their manual processes** behind the scenes.
- They **waited for leadership to realize the project wasn't working**.

And guess what? It **failed**.

The company **scrapped the AI system after just one year**, wasting millions of dollars. Had they communicated early on that the **system was designed to assist employees, not replace them**, they could have saved themselves a **fortune**.

Lesson learned? **If you don't address employee fears upfront, they will resist the change—passively or aggressively.**

---

2. The Fear of Incompetence – "I have no idea how to use this thing!"

The Cost of Ignoring Change Management

Picture this: A global **FMCG company** decides to roll out an **automated sales forecasting system** across its supply chain. The goal? **Reduce stockouts and overproduction** by using AI to predict demand more accurately.

But here's the problem:

- The frontline employees—who had been doing demand forecasting **manually for 20 years**—weren't given proper training.
- The new system was **complicated, full of jargon, and required multiple logins** (because, of course, every new system needs more passwords).
- Instead of making their lives easier, it **added stress** because they didn't know how to use it.

So, what did they do?

- They **kept using their old Excel sheets** behind the scenes.
- They **manually overrode AI predictions** with their own "gut feeling."
- They **blamed the system when things went wrong**.

Result? **The system was declared a failure, and the company went back to manual forecasting.**

The irony? The **technology was fine**. It was the **lack of training and change management** that doomed it.

Lesson learned? **If people don't feel competent with a new system, they will resist it—even if it's better than what they had before.**

3. Change Fatigue – "Oh great, another new system. Just what we needed."

Imagine working in **real estate**, where everything moves fast, and deals are closed over coffee meetings and handshakes. Then, one day, leadership decides to implement **a new digital property management system**—a fancy cloud-based tool designed to "streamline operations."

The employees had already **survived three major system changes in the last five years**, and now they were being asked to learn *another* one.

Their reaction?

- **"We just learned the last system! Why change again?"**
- **"This isn't going to last. Just wait it out."**
- **"I bet they'll switch to something else next year."**

And guess what? **They were right**.

Six months in, adoption rates were so low that the company **ditched the new system and reverted to the old one**. Millions of dollars wasted. Again.

Lesson learned? **If you keep changing systems without a clear reason and proper engagement, employees will assume every new initiative is temporary—and they'll ignore it.**

The Human Side of Digital Transformation: How to Make Change Stick

Now that we've explored *why* people resist change, let's talk about how to **overcome resistance** and make sure digital transformation actually works.

Here's what the best companies do right:

1. Make Employees Part of the Change (Not Just Victims of It)

- The best companies **involve employees early**—not just when the change is about to be implemented.
- Before rolling out new tech, they **gather feedback**, **address concerns**, and **co-create solutions**.

Example? **Amazon's warehouse automation.**

- Instead of blindsiding employees, Amazon **trained them early**, ensuring they saw robotics as a **tool to assist them**, not a job replacement strategy.

2. Invest in Training (No, Watching a 5-Minute Tutorial is NOT Enough)

- Employees should feel **competent and confident** with new technology.
- Training should be **hands-on, engaging, and ongoing**—not just a one-time PowerPoint presentation.

Example? **Airbnb's AI-powered customer service rollout.**

- Airbnb **gamified employee training**, making it fun and rewarding to learn the new AI system.
- Employees **competed in real-life AI use cases**, making them comfortable with automation instead of fearing it.

3. Change Shouldn't Feel Like Punishment

- Change should be framed as **an opportunity, not an obligation**.
- Companies that provide **incentives, recognition, and ongoing support** have **far higher adoption rates**.

Example? **Netflix's culture of innovation.**

- Netflix embraces change by **rewarding employees for experimenting with new tools** instead of punishing them for mistakes.

Final Thoughts: If You Ignore the People, You Lose the Battle

After **20 years in technology transformation**, I've seen the same mistake repeated **countless times**:

- Companies invest millions in **cutting-edge software**, but **nothing in change management**.
- Leaders assume that **employees will just "figure it out."** Spoiler alert: **they won't.**
- Employees, feeling ignored, **find ways to sabotage, resist, or outright reject the change**.

If you take one thing away from this chapter, let it be this:

People don't resist change because they're stubborn—they resist it because they're scared, unprepared, or just plain exhausted. If you don't address that, your digital transformation will fail.

So, the next time you hear someone say, *"We're rolling out a new system next month"*, ask them:

"And what's the plan for getting people to actually use it?"

Because if they don't have one, you already know how this story ends.

Chapter 3: The True Cost of Ignoring Change Management

How to Burn Millions of Dollars and Blame the IT Team

Technology Isn't the Problem—People Are, when it comes to adopting the digital change

Let me start with a hard truth: **technology doesn't fail—people do.**

Think about it. When was the last time a piece of software just *decided* to stop working out of spite? Never. But when employees **refuse to use it, sabotage it, or find ways to work around it**, that's when digital transformation efforts crash and burn.

And yet, companies continue to spend **billions** on cutting-edge tech while **investing almost nothing** in helping employees adapt. It's like buying a Ferrari for someone who doesn't know how to drive and expecting them to win a race.

Over the last **two decades**, I've watched this happen in **FMCG, pharma, construction, real estate, and beyond**. The same pattern repeats itself:

1. **Big investment in technology.**
2. **No investment in change management.**
3. **Employees hate the new system.**
4. **Leadership blames IT.**
5. **Millions of dollars wasted.**

Still skeptical? Let's take a look at some **real-world horror stories** of what happens when companies neglect change management.

FMCG Disaster: The Self-Sabotaging Supply Chain

Imagine a multinational **FMCG company** that decides to roll out a state-of-the-art **automated demand forecasting system**. The goal? **Reduce stockouts and overproduction** by using AI to predict customer demand.

Sounds smart, right?

Here's what actually happened:

- The **supply chain team** wasn't involved in the planning process.
- When the system launched, employees **didn't trust the AI predictions**.
- Instead of following the new system, employees **manually adjusted forecasts** using their *gut instinct*.
- The system, seeing these changes, assumed demand was fluctuating and **adjusted future predictions accordingly**.

The result?

- **Warehouses overflowed with unsellable stock**, while high-demand items ran out.
- The company lost **millions** in wasted inventory and missed sales.
- The system was **blamed, scrapped, and replaced**—even though it *would have worked fine* if people had actually used it.

Lesson? **If employees don't trust a system, they will find ways to break it—even unintentionally.**

Pharma Fiasco: The Regulatory Nightmare

Now, let's talk about **PharmaCorp**, a company that invested **$50 million** in a new **electronic document management system (EDMS)** to streamline **FDA compliance**.

The idea was simple:

- Automate regulatory documentation.
- Reduce human errors.
- Speed up approvals.

Here's what went wrong:

- **No one trained the regulatory affairs team.**
- Employees were overwhelmed and **kept using their old manual system**—even though it wasn't compliant anymore.
- The FDA audit uncovered **massive inconsistencies** between the new system and the old records.

The result?

- **Major compliance violations.**
- **Product recalls worth millions.**
- **Regulatory fines and reputational damage.**

The system itself was **perfectly fine**—the company just **never ensured employees knew how to use it.**

Lesson? **If your employees aren't trained properly, new systems will actually make things worse, not better.**

Real Estate Recklessness: The Ghost CRM

A leading **real estate firm** invested in a **high-end CRM (Customer Relationship Management) system** to help property agents track deals, leads, and client interactions.

Here's what happened instead:

- The sales team **hated the system** because it required **too much manual data entry**.
- They **ignored it completely** and kept **using WhatsApp and Excel** to track leads.
- Management, assuming the CRM was working, **made critical business decisions** based on its (non-existent) data.

The result?

- **Lost sales opportunities** because no one updated the CRM.
- **Mismatched client data**, leading to embarrassing mistakes.
- **The system was abandoned within a year**, after burning **millions of dollars**.

Lesson? **If employees don't see value in using a new system, they'll find a workaround.**

The Hidden Costs of Ignoring Change Management

Every time a digital transformation project fails, **companies blame the technology**. But the real culprit is always **lack of change management**.

Here's what failed transformations actually cost businesses:

1. Financial Losses (A.K.A. Burning Money for Fun)

- **Hershey's lost $150 million** when its ERP failed (because employees weren't trained).
- **Ford wasted $400 million** on a digital overhaul that no one adopted.
- **BBC burned $150 million** on a failed content management system that employees ignored.

Ignoring change management is like **lighting money on fire**—except less fun and with more Excel reports explaining why profits are down.

2. Employee Frustration (Or, How to Make Your Best People Quit)

- When companies force technology on employees **without support**, frustration skyrockets.
- Employees who **feel unheard and undervalued** either **resist change** or **leave**.
- The worst part? The most **experienced and valuable** employees often **quit first**.

3. Customer Impact (Because Clients Don't Care About Your Excuses)

- If a supply chain system fails, **customers get delayed orders**.
- If a CRM isn't used, **clients feel ignored**.
- If a compliance system is abandoned, **regulators come knocking**.

When internal chaos spills over into **customer experience**, **revenues drop** and **brand reputation takes a hit**.

How to Stop the Madness: Winning Change Management Strategies

If you don't want to be the next Hershey's or Ford, here's what you need to do:

1. Get Employees Involved Early

- Before rolling out new tech, ask employees:
    - *"What frustrates you about the current system?"*
    - *"What would make your job easier?"*
- Involve **end-users** in design and testing.

Example: **Amazon tests new warehouse systems with actual workers before full deployment.**

2. Communicate the "Why" Clearly

- Employees need to know:
    - *"How will this help you?"*
    - *"What problem is this solving?"*
    - *"What's in it for you?"*

Example: **Microsoft's culture shift under Satya Nadella worked because he made employees understand the purpose behind digital changes.**

3. Invest in Proper Training (Not Just a PowerPoint Presentation)

- Training should be:
    - Hands-on
    - Continuous
    - Adapted to different learning styles

Example: **Airbnb gamified AI training to make learning fun and engaging.**

4. Reward Early Adopters

- Create **incentives** for employees who embrace the change.
- Recognize and celebrate **small wins**.

Example: **Netflix rewards employees who experiment with new tools, fostering a culture of innovation.**

Final Thoughts: Change Management is the Key to Digital Success

Let me put it plainly: **Digital transformation isn't about technology—it's about people.**

Over the past **20 years**, I've seen brilliant systems fail because employees weren't engaged, and I've seen mediocre technology succeed because people **believed in it**.

So, before you invest millions in a new system, ask yourself:

"Do I have a plan to make sure my employees actually use it?"

If not, congratulations—you're about to waste a fortune.

Chapter 4: FMCG – Automation Without Adoption

How to Spend Millions on Tech and Still End Up with Excel Sheets

The FMCG Industry's Love-Hate Relationship with Digital Transformation

Fast-Moving Consumer Goods (FMCG) companies thrive on **speed, efficiency, and razor-thin margins**. They operate in a world where **one supply chain hiccup can mean empty supermarket shelves**, and a poorly timed product launch can mean **millions in lost sales**.

So naturally, these companies **love investing in technology** to stay ahead.

The problem? **Their employees don't.**

Despite investing billions in automation, AI, and predictive analytics, many FMCG companies **still struggle with digital adoption**. Why? Because they **ignore the human side of transformation**—and when people aren't on board, no amount of AI magic can save the day.

Let's explore some *real-life disasters* where FMCG companies **spent big on technology but forgot to bring their employees along for the ride**.

The ERP That Broke a Multinational Snack Giant

Meet **SnackCorp**, a global FMCG brand known for its wildly popular chips and biscuits. Looking to **modernize operations**, the company **invested $200 million in a state-of-the-art ERP system** to automate supply chain management.

The goal? **Seamless integration between factories, warehouses, and retailers.**

What actually happened?

- The system was designed **without consulting warehouse and factory workers**.
- The UI was so **complicated** that even IT specialists struggled to use it.
- Employees **refused to trust the automated forecasting system**, preferring their "tried-and-tested" manual calculations.
- Instead of improving efficiency, the system **caused massive delays**—orders piled up, deliveries were late, and stockouts became a daily nightmare.

The result?

- **Supermarkets pulled SnackCorp's products from shelves.**
- The **company lost millions in sales** within six months.
- After two years of struggles, the ERP was **abandoned**, and the company quietly returned to its **Excel-based system** (yes, really).

The lesson? **If employees don't trust a new system, they will find a way to bypass it.**

The AI Sales Prediction That Nobody Trusted

Next, we have **DairyDelight**, a leading dairy brand that decided to **leverage AI for demand forecasting**.

The idea was brilliant:

- Use **AI-powered analytics** to predict demand for milk, cheese, and yogurt.
- Prevent **waste by reducing overproduction**.
- Ensure **shelves were always stocked with exactly what customers wanted**.

What could possibly go wrong?

Well...

- The **sales team wasn't involved** in the AI implementation.
- When AI **predicted demand lower than what sales teams expected**, employees **manually overrode the system**.
- Distributors, skeptical of the new forecasts, **continued placing bulk orders "just in case."**

The result?

- **Warehouses flooded with unsold dairy products.**
- **Millions lost in expired goods** (and a lot of sour milk).
- The AI system was **blamed for "bad predictions"**—even though it was employees **who refused to follow the recommendations**.

The real issue? **The company never got employees to trust or understand the AI model.**

The Pharma Packaging Nightmare – When Automation Meets Resistance

Now, let's shift gears to the **pharmaceutical industry**, where compliance is everything.

A global **pharma company** decided to automate its **drug packaging process** with a **robotic system** designed to reduce human error and ensure FDA compliance.

Sounds like a great idea, right?

Except…

- The factory workers saw the new machines as **a threat to their jobs**.
- Instead of **collaborating with the automation**, they **found ways to slow it down**—claiming "technical issues" that didn't exist.
- Some even **deliberately entered incorrect data** to prove that the new system was unreliable.

The result?

- **Production delays skyrocketed.**
- The company **missed major product deadlines**.
- Leadership **scrapped the automation project**—blaming "technology limitations" (even though the real issue was **resistance from employees**).

Lesson? **If employees see new technology as the enemy, they will sabotage it—consciously or unconsciously.**

Why FMCG and Pharma Workers Resist Digital Transformation

So, why do FMCG and pharmaceutical employees fight change so much?

It all boils down to **three simple reasons**:

1. "This System Was Forced on Us."

Nobody likes being **told** to change—especially when they weren't included in the decision-making process.

Most digital transformation failures start with **executives choosing technology without consulting the people who will actually use it.**

Fix it: **Involve employees from day one.** Ask them:

- *What frustrates you about the current system?*
- *What would actually make your job easier?*

2. "I Don't Trust This New System."

FMCG and pharma workers rely on **experience and intuition** to make decisions. If a new system **contradicts their gut feeling**, they will ignore it.

Fix it: **Show them why the new system works.**

- Use **real-world examples** to prove that AI, automation, or ERP recommendations **are accurate**.
- Provide **small, low-risk trials** to build confidence.

3. "I'm Not Ready for This Change."

Most digital rollouts fail because **employees weren't trained properly**. A few PowerPoint slides and a company-wide email don't count as training.

Fix it: **Invest in proper training.**

- Hands-on workshops
- Peer-led learning sessions
- Gamified training programs

How to Get FMCG and Pharma Employees to Embrace Change

If you don't want to **waste millions** on technology that nobody uses, here's how to make change stick:

1. Make Employees Feel Like They Own the Change

Instead of **forcing** technology on employees, make them **part of the decision-making process**.

Example: **Unilever successfully rolled out a global supply chain AI system** by getting **warehouse staff, sales teams, and factory workers involved in the pilot phase.**

2. Give People a Reason to Trust the System

Trust doesn't happen automatically—it needs to be earned.

Example: **Procter & Gamble's predictive analytics system** initially faced resistance, but after **executives showed how it improved forecasting accuracy**, employees **started trusting the AI recommendations.**

3. Offer Incentives for Early Adoption

People love rewards. Offer **bonuses, recognition, or career growth opportunities** for employees who **actively use and champion the new system**.

Example: **Nestlé rewarded employees** who successfully transitioned to their new ERP system by **giving them leadership roles in future tech projects.**

Final Thoughts: If You Ignore Change Management, Expect Failure

FMCG and pharmaceutical companies are **masters of efficiency**—but **terrible at change management**.

Here's the **brutal reality**:

- **Technology alone never guarantees success.**
- **If employees don't trust, understand, or feel included in the change, they will resist it.**
- **Digital transformation is 80% about people and 20% about technology.**

So before you invest millions in **AI, ERP, automation, or analytics**, ask yourself:

"Do my employees actually want and understand this change?"

Because if they don't, congratulations—you just bought yourself a **very expensive** (and totally unused) **software license.**

Chapter 5: Construction – The Digital Blueprint That Never Took Off

Why a $10 Million Software Ended Up as an Expensive Paperweight

The Construction Industry's Struggle with Digital Transformation

Construction is one of the **oldest and most traditional industries** in the world. For centuries, buildings were designed with **hand-drawn blueprints**, project timelines were managed with **clipboards**, and contractors relied on **gut instinct rather than data analytics**.

Then came **digital transformation**, promising to revolutionize construction with:

- **Building Information Modeling (BIM)** for smarter planning
- **AI-powered scheduling** to reduce delays
- **Cloud-based project management tools** to improve efficiency
- **Drones and automation** to speed up site inspections

Sounds great, right?

Well, there's just **one problem: construction workers, engineers, and project managers don't exactly love change.**

In my two decades working on **technology transformation projects**, I've seen construction firms **burn millions on digital initiatives that never get used**. Why? Because they **ignored the human factor**.

Let's look at some *real-world disasters* where **digital transformation in construction failed—not because of bad technology, but because of resistance to change.**

The BIM Implementation That Became a Costly Disaster

Meet **BuildMax**, a major construction company that decided to invest **$10 million in a Building Information Modeling (BIM) system**. The idea was simple:

- **Digitize blueprints** and create a **centralized 3D model**.
- Improve **coordination between architects, engineers, and contractors**.
- Reduce **costly mistakes and delays**.

What could possibly go wrong?

Here's what actually happened:

- The **senior engineers hated the system** because they were used to traditional blueprints.
- The **construction managers didn't trust the digital model** and continued using **hand-drawn plans**.
- The **on-site teams ignored the BIM data**, leading to **costly rework** when mistakes weren't caught early.

The result?

- The project **ran $25 million over budget** due to errors that **BIM could have prevented**—if anyone had actually used it.
- After two years of frustration, the company **quietly abandoned BIM**, writing off the entire investment.

Lesson? **If the people using the technology don't trust it, it doesn't matter how good it is.**

The AI-Powered Scheduling Tool That No One Used

Next, we have **SkyHigh Constructions**, which wanted to **eliminate project delays** by using an **AI-powered scheduling system**.

The system promised to:

- **Predict delays before they happened.**
- **Optimize worker schedules** based on weather, material availability, and productivity.
- **Reduce idle time and improve efficiency.**

Here's what went wrong:

- **Project managers felt threatened**, fearing the AI system would replace their decision-making.
- **Workers ignored automated schedules** and followed the "usual way" of doing things.
- **Site supervisors manually overrode AI predictions** because they didn't trust the technology.

The result?

- The system was **branded a failure**, even though **the real failure was employee adoption.**
- The company **went back to Excel spreadsheets**—because *"it worked just fine before."*

Lesson? **Technology can't fix inefficiencies if employees refuse to change their habits.**

The Smart Helmet That Nobody Wore

A **major real estate developer** invested in **AI-powered smart helmets** for on-site workers. The helmets were designed to:

- **Monitor worker fatigue** and prevent accidents.
- **Provide real-time safety alerts** through augmented reality.
- **Track worker location** to ensure site compliance.

Sounds revolutionary, right?

Except…

- Workers **hated the helmets** because they felt like *"big brother was watching."*
- Some **intentionally disabled the smart sensors** to avoid being monitored.
- Within a few months, the **helmets were sitting unused in storage rooms**.

The result?

- **$5 million wasted** on cutting-edge safety gear that no one wanted to use.
- The company **went back to traditional safety measures** after employee complaints.

Lesson? **If employees see technology as surveillance rather than support, they will reject it.**

Why Construction Workers Resist Digital Transformation

Unlike industries where employees work behind a desk, construction workers are **on the ground, solving real-world problems**. They rely on **experience, instinct, and hands-on skills**—not data-driven dashboards.

Here's why they often resist digital transformation:

1. "This Tech Was Forced on Us."

Construction workers are **used to practical, hands-on problem-solving**. When they're suddenly asked to **rely on a digital system** they don't understand, their first reaction is: *"Why are we doing this?"*

Fix it: **Involve workers in the decision-making process.**

- Ask **site managers and engineers for feedback** before rolling out new tech.
- Run **pilot projects** before full implementation.

2. "I Don't Trust a Computer to Do My Job."

Imagine telling a **construction foreman with 30 years of experience** that an AI system will now **optimize work schedules**.

His response? *"I've been doing this for decades. I don't need a computer to tell me how to build a bridge."*

Fix it: **Show proof that the technology works.**

- Demonstrate **small wins** before expecting full adoption.
- Provide **real-time comparisons** between traditional methods and the new system.

3. "I Don't Have Time to Learn This."

Construction projects run on **tight deadlines**. Expecting workers to take time out of their day to **learn a complicated new tool** without proper training is a recipe for failure.

Fix it: **Invest in simple, hands-on training.**

- Offer **on-site training workshops** rather than just online tutorials.
- Assign **digital champions** on each project site to help workers adapt.

How to Get Construction Teams to Embrace Digital Transformation

If you want digital tools to actually **work** in construction, here's what you need to do:

1. Make Technology a Tool, Not a Threat

Employees will **always resist change if they feel like technology is replacing them**.

Example: **A leading construction firm successfully introduced AI scheduling** by positioning it as a **"decision support tool"** **rather than an automation replacement.**

2. Reward Adoption, Don't Punish Resistance

Instead of **forcing** digital adoption, **reward employees who embrace it**.

Example: **A real estate firm gave performance bonuses** to site supervisors who successfully implemented a digital project management tool.

3. Keep It Simple

Construction workers aren't **data scientists**—they don't want a complicated interface.

Example: **A global construction company increased mobile app adoption** by designing a **simple, user-friendly dashboard** with one-click reporting.

Final Thoughts: Digital Transformation in Construction is About People, Not Just Tech

Construction companies **love investing in new technology**, but they **often forget about the people using it**.

Here's the **harsh reality**:

- **No digital system will work if employees don't trust it.**
- **If the tech is too complicated, workers will ignore it.**
- **Forcing technology without proper training is a guaranteed failure.**

So before investing millions in **AI-powered scheduling, drone inspections, or smart safety gear**, ask yourself:

"Have we actually talked to the people who will use this?"

Because if the answer is **no**, you're about to waste a lot of money on tech that will **sit in storage collecting dust**.

Chapter 6: Pharma – Compliance and Chaos

How to Spend Millions on a System That Nobody Uses and Still Fail an FDA Audit

---

The Pharma Industry's Love-Hate Relationship with Digital Transformation

Pharmaceutical companies are in a **constant battle with time, regulations, and innovation**. They operate in a world where:

- **Compliance failures** mean billion-dollar fines.
- **Supply chain hiccups** can delay life-saving drugs.
- **R&D is unpredictable**, and one failed trial can tank an entire company.

So, naturally, pharma companies **love investing in cutting-edge technology** to stay ahead.

The problem? **Their employees don't.**

If you've ever seen a **regulatory affairs team panic when asked to switch from paper to digital records**, or a **lab technician look at an AI-powered research tool like it's an alien spacecraft**, you'll understand exactly what I mean.

And while pharma loves technology on paper, **most digital transformations fail spectacularly** because they **ignore the people who actually have to use the systems**.

Let's dive into some **real-world disasters** where pharma companies spent **millions on digital solutions—only to end up with bigger problems than before.**

The FDA Compliance System That Nobody Used

Meet **MediPharm**, a global pharmaceutical giant that needed to modernize its **regulatory documentation system**.

The old system?

- A **patchwork of spreadsheets, emails, and physical documents** spread across different departments.
- Data was **manually entered** (with plenty of errors).
- FDA audits were **a nightmare**—taking weeks to pull all the required documentation together.

So, the company decided to **invest $50 million in an AI-powered compliance management system** that would:

- **Automatically track regulatory changes.**
- **Ensure all documentation was up to date.**
- **Generate audit reports in seconds.**

Brilliant, right?

Except…

- **Nobody trained the employees properly** on how to use it.
- The system required **meticulous data entry**, which employees **found frustrating and time-consuming**.
- Some workers **continued using their old manual tracking methods** in parallel, creating **conflicting records**.

Then came the **FDA audit**.

The auditors asked for specific compliance reports. The regulatory affairs team confidently logged into their new system—only to find that **half the required data was missing** because employees hadn't been entering it properly.

The result?

- **Mass panic.**

- **\$10 million fine for compliance failures.**
- **Employees blamed the system, even though the real issue was poor adoption.**

Lesson? **A compliance system is only useful if people actually use it—and use it correctly.**

The AI Drug Discovery Tool That Nobody Trusted

Let's move to another example—**a mid-sized biotech company** that wanted to **speed up drug discovery** using **AI-powered data analytics**.

The idea?

- Use AI to **analyze clinical trial data** faster.
- Predict **which drug formulations had the highest success rates**.
- Reduce **failed experiments** and save time.

Reality?

- **Scientists didn't trust AI predictions**, preferring their **own expertise and instincts**.
- **Some even manipulated data** to make AI recommendations align with their expectations.
- AI flagged this inconsistency, leading to **even more confusion and frustration**.

The result?

- The AI tool was **abandoned after a year**.
- The company **went back to traditional research methods**.
- Millions of dollars were **wasted on a system no one believed in.**

Lesson? **If employees don't trust the system, they will find ways to work around it—even if it means sabotaging digital transformation.**

The Pharmaceutical Supply Chain Meltdown

Next, let's talk about **a major vaccine manufacturer** that implemented a **blockchain-based supply chain tracking system**.

The goal?

- **Track raw materials** in real-time.
- **Prevent counterfeit drugs** from entering the market.
- Improve **logistics efficiency** for global vaccine distribution.

What went wrong?

- The **warehouse staff had no idea how blockchain worked** and found the interface **confusing**.
- Many shipments were **not properly logged**, leading to **missing inventory records**.
- **Logistics managers bypassed the system** by keeping their own **spreadsheet backups** (which they trusted more).

The result?

- **A major supply chain disruption**—vaccine shipments went missing, and deliveries were delayed.
- The company faced **backlash from regulators and customers**.
- After millions in losses, the blockchain system was **scrapped** and replaced with… you guessed it—**a manual tracking process**.

Lesson? **If employees don't understand the technology, they will default to old habits—even if it means ignoring a multi-million-dollar investment.**

Why Pharma Employees Resist Digital Transformation

Pharmaceutical professionals are **highly skilled experts**—scientists, regulatory specialists, and engineers. They've spent **years mastering their fields** using established processes.

So, when a company suddenly says, *"Hey, here's a new AI tool that does your job differently"*, their first reaction is: **"Why should I trust this?"**

Here's why they resist digital transformation:

1. "This Isn't How We've Always Done It."

Pharma is an **industry built on tradition and precision**. Employees are trained to **follow strict protocols**—and digital disruption **feels like chaos** to them.

Fix it: **Show them the long-term benefits and back it with real-world results.**

- Give **examples of how the technology has improved efficiency in other pharma companies**.
- Start with **small-scale implementations before a full rollout**.

2. "I Don't Trust a Machine Over My Expertise."

Scientists and regulatory experts **don't want AI making decisions for them—especially when their work involves public health and safety**.

Fix it: **Position technology as a decision-support tool, not a replacement.**

- Emphasize **human oversight** in AI-driven decisions.
- Ensure that **employees still have control over critical choices**.

3. "This System is Too Complicated."

If a digital tool **adds extra steps** or feels like **more work**, employees **won't use it—no matter how powerful it is**.

Fix it: **Simplify user interfaces and workflows.**

- Conduct **hands-on training** instead of just sending a 50-page manual.
- Design systems that **integrate seamlessly into existing workflows**.

How to Make Digital Transformation Work in Pharma

If you don't want your **multi-million-dollar investment to become an expensive failure**, here's how to make sure pharma employees **actually adopt new technology**:

1. Get Scientists, Regulatory Teams, and Supply Chain Managers Involved Early

- Before rolling out a new system, **get input from end-users**.

- Test the system in **real-life workflows** before full implementation.

Example: **Pfizer successfully adopted an AI-powered drug research tool** by **co-developing it with their scientists** rather than just handing it over.

2. Provide Incentives for Digital Adoption

- Reward employees who **embrace the new system**.
- Recognize **early adopters** as digital transformation champions.

Example: **Novartis increased AI adoption by rewarding scientists whose AI-assisted research led to new discoveries.**

3. Make Training Engaging (Not Just a Boring PowerPoint)

- Use **gamified learning** and real-world scenarios.
- Provide **hands-on workshops and mentorship programs**.

Example: **A major biotech company improved compliance system adoption** by turning training into **interactive case studies** rather than generic tutorials.

Final Thoughts: Digital Transformation is a People Problem, Not a Technology Problem

Pharma companies spend billions on **AI, automation, and cloud solutions**, but **most digital initiatives fail because they ignore the people using them.**

Here's the brutal truth:

- **A system that nobody trusts is a system that won't be used.**

- **If employees don't see value in digital tools, they will default to old habits.**
- **Successful digital transformation is 80% people and 20% technology.**

So, before investing millions in **a new compliance tool, AI research system, or blockchain supply chain tracker**, ask yourself:

"Do my employees actually understand and trust this change?"

Because if they don't, congratulations—you just bought **the world's most expensive software that nobody will use.**

Chapter 7: Real Estate – Smart Systems, Stubborn Mindsets

How to Spend Millions on a Property Tech Revolution That Nobody Wanted

The Real Estate Industry's Reluctance to Change

Real estate is an industry built on **relationships, negotiations, and handshakes.** For decades, deals have been **closed over coffee meetings** rather than dashboards, and sales strategies have revolved around **gut instinct rather than data analytics**.

Then came **PropTech (Property Technology)**—a wave of digital transformation that promised to revolutionize real estate with:

- **AI-powered pricing algorithms** to determine the best market rates.
- **Blockchain-based property transactions** to eliminate paperwork.
- **Smart property management systems** for seamless maintenance and tenant management.
- **Virtual reality (VR) home tours** to save time and money.

Sounds like a real estate agent's dream, right?

Except… most agents, landlords, and developers **didn't want it.**

Despite billions invested in **digital platforms, AI tools, and automation**, many real estate professionals **still prefer spreadsheets, phone calls, and handwritten notes.**

Why? Because **no one took the time to get them on board**.

Let's explore some *real-world failures* where real estate companies **bet big on digital transformation—only to end up with frustrated employees, abandoned systems, and wasted millions.**

The CRM That Became an Expensive Digital Ghost Town

Meet **UrbanHomes**, a real estate firm that decided to **digitize its entire sales process** with a cutting-edge **CRM (Customer Relationship Management) system**.

The system promised to:

- **Track client interactions automatically.**
- **Send AI-driven property recommendations** to potential buyers.
- **Simplify follow-ups with automated reminders.**

What actually happened?

- The **sales team ignored it** because **manual data entry was a nightmare**.
- Some agents **continued tracking leads on paper or in WhatsApp chats**.
- The few who *did* use the CRM found **incomplete or outdated information**, making the system unreliable.

The result?

- **Management thought leads were being followed up—when they weren't.**
- Agents **complained that the CRM slowed them down**, rather than helping them.
- After a year, **the system was quietly abandoned, and the company went back to spreadsheets.**

Lesson? **A CRM is only useful if agents actually use it. Otherwise, it's just an expensive digital filing cabinet.**

The Smart Building Management System That Nobody Logged Into

Next, we have **Skyline Properties**, a luxury real estate company that spent **$20 million** developing a **smart building management system** for its rental properties.

The system was designed to:

- **Automate maintenance requests** with AI-powered predictions.
- **Allow tenants to pay rent digitally** through a seamless app.
- **Integrate IoT sensors** to optimize energy efficiency.

Sounds futuristic, right?

Here's what went wrong:

- **Property managers weren't trained properly**, so they didn't know how to use half the features.
- Tenants found the app **complicated**, so they **continued calling the property office instead of using the system**.
- **Maintenance teams didn't trust AI diagnostics**, so they **ignored automated repair alerts**.

The result?

- **Tenant complaints skyrocketed** because nobody was actually using the system.
- **Property managers blamed the tech**, rather than their own lack of training.

- The company **spent millions reverting to manual processes**—even though the smart system could have worked fine.

Lesson? **If people don't understand or trust a system, they won't use it—no matter how advanced it is.**

The AI-Powered Property Pricing Model That Everyone Ignored

Let's move on to **MetroRealty**, a large property investment firm that wanted to use **AI to determine property pricing.**

The idea?

- AI would **analyze market trends** and **predict the best price for every listing.**
- Agents would **stop relying on gut instinct** and start using **data-driven insights.**
- The company would **maximize sales and rental income**.

What actually happened?

- The **agents hated it** because the AI often **recommended lower prices than what they expected**.
- Some agents **deliberately ignored AI pricing** and listed properties at their own rates.
- **When properties took longer to sell, AI was blamed**, even though it was the human agents who had overridden its recommendations.

The result?

- **Inconsistent pricing strategies** across the company.
- **Clients lost trust** because different agents were offering conflicting advice.

- After a year, **MetroRealty quietly ditched the AI model and went back to "expert intuition."**

Lesson? **If employees don't believe in the technology, they will find ways to ignore or override it.**

Why Real Estate Professionals Resist Digital Transformation

Unlike industries where everything is **data-driven**, real estate is still **heavily relationship-based**. Agents, property managers, and landlords rely on **personal connections and experience**—not just software.

Here's why they resist digital change:

1. "I Don't Have Time to Enter Data."

Most real estate professionals are **on the go**, meeting clients, closing deals, and managing properties. If technology **slows them down** rather than making their lives easier, they won't use it.

Fix it: **Make digital tools seamless and mobile-friendly.**

- Reduce **manual data entry** as much as possible.
- Integrate **AI assistants** to capture key information automatically.

2. "I Trust My Experience More Than an Algorithm."

Real estate agents **pride themselves on intuition**—they've spent years learning **how to read the market, negotiate deals, and close sales.**

Fix it: **Position AI as a supporting tool, not a replacement.**

- Show them **case studies** of how AI pricing has improved sales.

- Give agents **control**—allow them to **adjust AI recommendations** rather than forcing them to accept automated decisions.

3. "Clients Want a Personal Touch—Not Just an App."

Real estate is **about relationships**. Many professionals worry that **too much automation will remove the personal element of buying or renting a home.**

Fix it: **Use digital tools to enhance—not replace—human interaction.**

- Automate **boring admin tasks**, so agents have more time for **high-value conversations.**
- Offer **hybrid options**—where clients can start online but still get **personal guidance from an agent.**

How to Make Digital Transformation Work in Real Estate

If you don't want to **waste millions on tech that nobody uses**, here's how to make sure **real estate professionals actually adopt new digital tools**:

1. Involve Agents and Property Managers Early

- **Don't force technology on them**—involve them in **testing and feedback.**
- Let them **see the benefits firsthand** before making big changes.

Example: **A leading property firm successfully introduced AI pricing by running a "human vs. AI" pricing challenge—proving that AI was more accurate.**

2. Keep It Simple (Seriously, Nobody Wants a Complicated System)

- Real estate professionals **aren't data analysts**—make interfaces **easy and intuitive**.
- **Reduce clicks, forms, and unnecessary features.**

Example: **Zillow increased adoption of its AI pricing tool by making recommendations visible in just two clicks.**

3. Reward Early Adopters and Provide Real Training

- **Offer incentives** for agents who use new systems effectively.
- **Train people properly**—not just with a manual, but through **interactive workshops.**

Example: **A real estate company increased CRM adoption by offering commission bonuses to agents who actively used the system.**

Final Thoughts: If You Ignore the Human Element, Your Tech Investment is Wasted

Real estate **loves the idea of digital transformation**—but the reality is messy.

Here's the truth:

- **A system that agents don't use is just an expensive failure.**
- **If technology doesn't fit into daily workflows, people will ignore it.**
- **Digital transformation should enhance relationships—not replace them.**

So before spending millions on **smart property management, AI pricing, or a CRM system**, ask yourself:

"Will my employees and agents actually use this?"

Because if the answer is **no**, congratulations—you just bought **the most expensive software that will sit unused on their laptops.**

Chapter 8: Change Management Frameworks That Work

Why Sending an Email Saying "Please Use the New System" is Not a Strategy

Why Change Management is the Secret Sauce of Digital Transformation

Imagine you've just spent **millions on a cutting-edge technology** that promises to revolutionize your business. It's got all the bells and whistles—AI-driven analytics, cloud-powered efficiency, and a dashboard that looks like something out of a sci-fi movie.

You roll it out with a grand announcement:

- A company-wide email with the subject line: **"Exciting Changes Coming Your Way!"**
- A mandatory **45-minute training webinar** where an IT guy drones on about system capabilities.
- A follow-up email: *"As of Monday, we will no longer be using the old system. Please migrate everything to the new platform. Thanks!"*

And then... crickets.

- Employees ignore the system.
- Some try to use it but give up after a frustrating first attempt.
- A few rebel quietly by **keeping their old methods running in the background.**
- Managers start blaming IT, while IT blames employees for "not embracing innovation."

Sound familiar?

That's because **most digital transformation failures happen due to bad (or nonexistent) change management**. You can't just introduce new technology and expect people to magically adopt it. **Change needs to be led, not just announced.**

Let's explore some *real-world disasters* where companies **ignored proper change management frameworks**—and paid the price.

The FMCG ERP Disaster – A Lesson in "Figure It Out Yourself"

Meet **SnackFast**, a global FMCG company that sells snacks in over 50 countries. Business was booming, but their **supply chain was a mess**—orders were delayed, inventory tracking was inconsistent, and warehouses often ran out of bestsellers.

The solution? A **$100 million ERP (Enterprise Resource Planning) system** that would:

- **Automate inventory management**
- **Predict demand more accurately**
- **Make the supply chain run like a well-oiled machine**

Great plan! Except… they **forgot about the people using the system.**

What went wrong?

- **Zero employee input during implementation.** The system was built with **no feedback from the actual warehouse and logistics teams** who would be using it daily.
- **No real training.** Employees were given **a PDF manual** (*because obviously, everyone loves reading 100-page instruction guides*).
- **No leadership involvement.** Managers simply assumed their teams would "just figure it out."

The result?

- Warehouse teams **ignored the ERP system** and continued using their old spreadsheets.
- Supply chain confusion actually **got worse** because data was split between the old and new systems.
- **$100 million wasted**—and the company quietly reverted to its old way of doing things.

Lesson? **You can't force technology on employees without preparing them for it.**

The Pharma Compliance Catastrophe – When Resistance Wins

Now, let's talk about **MediLife**, a pharmaceutical company that implemented a new **regulatory compliance system** to streamline **FDA reporting**.

The old way?

- **Manual documentation**—a mix of Excel, paper records, and email chains.
- **Painfully slow audits** that took weeks to compile compliance data.

So, MediLife invested **$50 million** in a **digital compliance system** that would:

- **Automate compliance tracking**
- **Reduce errors**
- **Prepare reports at the click of a button**

But guess what? **Nobody used it.**

Why?

- **The regulatory affairs team wasn't consulted.** The system was designed by IT and leadership, **without input from the people actually doing compliance work.**
- **No change champions.** Employees didn't have **a go-to person** to answer their concerns, so they just **stuck with the old system.**
- **Punishment instead of motivation.** Leadership got frustrated and **threatened employees with consequences if they didn't use the system**—which only **increased resistance.**

The result?

- Employees **secretly continued using their Excel sheets.**
- The company **failed a major FDA audit** because the new system had incomplete data.
- The entire project **was scrapped after two years of frustration.**

Lesson? **People don't resist change—they resist being forced into something they don't understand or trust.**

So, What Actually Works? Change Management That Makes Sense

If you want **people to actually use new technology**, you need a structured approach. Here are some of the **best change management frameworks** that successful companies use.

1. The ADKAR Model – Because People Need Steps, Not Surprises

ADKAR is a **simple, human-centered framework** that helps employees move through change **one step at a time:**

- **A**wareness – Do employees understand *why* the change is happening?
- **D**esire – Do they actually *want* to use the new system?
- **K**nowledge – Have they been trained properly?
- **A**bility – Do they feel **confident** using the new system?
- **R**einforcement – Is there ongoing support so they don't revert to old habits?

Example: **An FMCG company successfully rolled out AI-driven sales forecasting** by:

- Explaining **why AI would make sales teams' jobs easier (Awareness & Desire)**
- Running **interactive training workshops (Knowledge & Ability)**
- Assigning **digital adoption coaches to support employees (Reinforcement)**

Result? **95% of sales teams adopted AI forecasting within a year.**

---

2. Kotter's 8-Step Change Model – Because Change Needs Leadership

John Kotter's model focuses on **leading change from the top-down and bottom-up**:

1. **Create urgency** – Why does this change need to happen now?
2. **Build a guiding coalition** – Who are your change champions?
3. **Form a strategic vision** – What does success look like?
4. **Communicate the vision** – Make sure everyone understands the goal.

5. **Remove obstacles** – Address employee concerns and barriers.
6. **Create short-term wins** – Celebrate small successes.
7. **Sustain acceleration** – Keep pushing forward.
8. **Institute change** – Make it part of company culture.

Example: **A pharmaceutical company successfully introduced a cloud-based R&D collaboration tool** by:

- Creating **a compelling case for change (urgency & vision)**
- Training **key scientists first (guiding coalition)**
- Celebrating **early successes (short-term wins)**

Result? **The company saw a 40% increase in research collaboration within a year.**

Final Thoughts: Change Management is the Secret Ingredient for Digital Success

Here's the harsh reality:

- **Technology doesn't fail—people fail to adopt it.**
- **If employees don't see value in a new system, they won't use it.**
- **If leadership doesn't lead the change, resistance will win.**

So, before you roll out **your next digital transformation project**, ask yourself:

- **Do employees actually want this change?**
- **Have we trained them properly?**
- **Do they feel supported, or just ordered around?**

Because if your entire strategy is **"just launch the system and hope for the best,"** you might as well start preparing for **why it will fail.**

The good news? **When you get change management right, digital transformation works.**

The bad news? **If you ignore it, congratulations—you've just bought the world's most expensive software that nobody will use.**

Chapter 9: Leadership's Role in Digital Success – The Captain of the Digital Ship

Introduction: The Captain Who Forgot the Map

Imagine you're on a luxury cruise ship. It's state-of-the-art, equipped with the latest technology—self-navigating systems, real-time weather tracking, AI-driven hospitality services. Everything seems perfect. But there's one small issue: the captain has no idea how to use any of it.

As a result, the ship is veering off course, the crew is confused, and the passengers—who were promised a smooth, tech-enhanced journey—are now doubting their decision to board. Chaos ensues.

Welcome to digital transformation without effective leadership.

Leaders often believe that implementing new technology is like buying a fancy yacht—just plug it in, and it will sail smoothly. But digital transformation is not a self-driving Tesla. It's more like piloting an aircraft: you need skilled hands, clear communication, and a team that trusts the captain.

In this chapter, we'll explore how leaders can make—or break—digital transformation. And because leadership mistakes are often best illustrated with real-world disasters, we'll dive into FMCG, pharma, and other industries where leaders either steered the ship safely—or ran it into an iceberg.

1. The "We Bought the Tech, Why Isn't It Working?" Syndrome

One of the biggest leadership mistakes in digital transformation is assuming that **buying the latest technology equals success**. It's like a CEO buying a Formula 1 car and expecting to win races without hiring a driver.

Case Study: The FMCG ERP Nightmare

A global FMCG company invested **millions** in a cutting-edge ERP system to streamline supply chain management. The tech was **flawless**—at least on paper. The problem?

- The CEO saw it as an IT project, not a business transformation.
- Middle managers were never trained on how to use it effectively.
- Factory workers, who had been using Excel for decades, were handed a **complex new interface overnight** with no training.

Result? The company **missed deliveries, orders were duplicated or lost**, and the entire system became an expensive **digital paperweight**. Employees started calling it **"The Titanic"**—big, expensive, and destined to sink.

Lesson Learned:

Leadership isn't just about buying tech. It's about **ensuring people understand, accept, and embrace it**. A system is only as good as the people using it.

2. The Pharma Disaster: When Leadership Forgot to Listen

Case Study: The Compliance Catastrophe

A large pharmaceutical firm decided to digitize its **compliance and regulatory reporting** system. Sounds great, right? But there was one problem—nobody **asked the employees** how they currently worked or what they needed.

- Senior leadership forced the rollout with **zero input** from the regulatory teams.
- The new system had **no flexibility** for real-world exceptions.
- Employees, desperate to meet deadlines, **created Excel workarounds** instead of using the new system.

When regulators visited, they found a **mess of half-digital, half-paper compliance reports**. The company was slapped with **millions in fines** for non-compliance. The CEO, in a panic, asked IT why the system failed. The answer? **"Because people didn't use it."**

Lesson Learned:

Leadership isn't just about choosing technology—it's about **engaging the people who will use it**. Ask, listen, iterate.

3. The "Just Do It" Leadership Style That Backfired

Some leaders believe that once they declare a digital transformation, it's **as good as done**. "We're going digital!" they announce, expecting instant change. But employees aren't widgets; they don't transform with a simple **Ctrl+Alt+Del**.

Case Study: The CEO vs. the Sales Team (FMCG again!)

A leading FMCG company implemented a **new AI-powered sales forecasting tool**. The CEO, convinced of its brilliance, made it **mandatory** for all sales teams. The tool required **daily data entry**, but sales reps—who were always on the move—hated it.

- They saw **no personal benefit** in using it.
- The app was **glitchy and slow on mobile**.
- Their manager **measured performance based on app usage, not actual sales**.

So what did they do? **They faked the data.**

The AI model, trained on **junk inputs**, **started making wildly inaccurate forecasts**. One region **accidentally overproduced inventory by 400%**, causing millions in losses. The CEO was furious. The sales teams shrugged: **"You wanted us to use the system. We did."**

Lesson Learned:

Technology needs to work **for employees, not just for leadership metrics**. If they don't see value, they won't use it properly.

4. What Good Leadership Looks Like in Digital Transformation

1. Lead from the Front, Not the Boardroom

Great leaders don't just approve budgets and disappear. They **actively participate** in the change process.

Example: A pharma CEO joined training sessions alongside employees when rolling out a digital R&D system. Seeing leadership embrace change **boosted adoption rates by 70%**.

2. Speak Human, Not Corporate

Avoid robotic corporate announcements:

1. **We are leveraging AI-driven synergies to optimize workflow efficiencies."**
2. **We're making your job easier by automating the boring stuff."**

People respond to **clear, relatable messaging**.

3. Find and Empower Change Champions

Every company has employees who **love** new tech. Find them, empower them, and let them **influence** their peers. Change spreads **faster through trust than authority**.

---

5. The Humorous Side of Change Resistance

Let's face it—people are **hilariously predictable** when faced with new technology. Here are some classic reactions:

- **The Veteran Skeptic:** *"We've always done it this way."*
- **The IT Guy:** *"This would have worked if you'd consulted us first."*
- **The Accidental Saboteur:** *"I clicked something, and now everything is gone."*
- **The Fake User:** *"Sure, I use the new system… when my boss is watching."*

Understanding these personas helps **leaders anticipate resistance** and tackle it with empathy and humor.

Conclusion: From Captain to Coach

A digital transformation leader isn't a dictator **("Use this system or else!")** but a **coach**—someone who inspires, trains, and supports their team. The best digital leaders:

- **Involve employees early**
- **Make changes practical and beneficial**
- **Train and support their teams continuously**
- **Encourage a culture where mistakes lead to learning, not punishment**

Because at the end of the day, digital transformation isn't just about **technology**.

It's about **people.**

And people don't resist **change**. They resist **being changed without a say.**

Final Thought:

The next time you embark on a digital transformation journey, ask yourself: **Are you leading it, or just watching from the bridge?**

Because a ship without an engaged captain doesn't just drift.

It **sinks**.

Chapter 10: Building a Change-Ready Culture – The Digital Gym Membership Problem

Introduction: The Digital Gym Membership Dilemma

Ever signed up for a **gym membership in January**, determined to get fit? The first week, you hit the gym daily. By February, you're down to once a week. By March… well, you still have the membership, but you're just donating money to the gym.

Digital transformation is exactly like a gym membership.

Companies eagerly invest in **new technology**, announce their **big transformation**, and expect everyone to **magically adopt it**. But within months, employees **quietly revert** to their old ways—just like people who stop going to the gym but keep telling themselves, *"I'll start again next Monday."*

So, how do you **build a culture** where people don't just sign up for change but **stick with it**?

Let's dive into some hilarious, painful, and eye-opening lessons from **FMCG, pharma, and beyond**, where companies either nailed cultural transformation—or ended up on the corporate version of a failed diet.

1. The "Launch and Ghost" Leadership Style

Case Study: The FMCG Tech Graveyard

A global **FMCG company** rolled out an AI-powered sales dashboard, designed to predict customer trends and improve marketing campaigns. The launch event was a spectacle—CEO speeches, fireworks (okay, maybe just PowerPoint animations), and free company-branded mugs.

Excitement was high.

But then…

- **No follow-up training** – Employees didn't know how to use it.
- **No incentives to use it** – The old system was easier.
- **No leadership involvement** – Executives never logged into the dashboard themselves.

Result? **Within six months, the fancy AI dashboard was as abandoned as a treadmill in mid-February.**

Lesson Learned:

Culture isn't built in a launch event. It's built **through daily habits, reinforcement, and leadership leading by example**.

2. The Pharma Documentation Disaster

Case Study: The Unread User Manual

A major **pharmaceutical company** invested millions in a **new digital documentation system** to ensure compliance with global regulations.

There was just one problem.

- The system was **designed by IT with zero input from employees.**
- It **required 15 clicks** to complete what used to take 2.
- The user manual was a **100-page PDF** (which, of course, **nobody read**).

What did employees do?

- They **stuck to using their old Excel sheets**, emailing documents back and forth.
- When audits happened, they **frantically uploaded months of paperwork overnight** to make it look like they were using the system.
- Regulators saw the **digital timestamps**, realized it was all fake, and fined the company heavily.

Lesson Learned:

Digital transformation is **not just about tech—it's about people**. If the system is harder to use than the old way, people will always **work around it.**

3. The "We're Too Busy for This" Problem

Imagine you're drowning in emails, deadlines, and meetings. Now, your company rolls out **a brand-new software system** and expects you to learn it on top of everything else.

You think, *"Sure, I'll do this… right after I finish my actual work."*

And that's how digital transformation dies.

Case Study: The Sales Rebellion (FMCG Again!)

An FMCG company forced their sales team to start using a **new mobile app** to track customer visits. The idea was great—real-time data, better reporting, all that good stuff.

The problem?

- The app was **slow** and **buggy**.
- The sales reps were already overworked and had **no time to learn it**.
- The old method (texting updates to their manager) **worked just fine for them**.

Within weeks, the **sales team collectively "forgot" their login passwords** (a classic move in corporate rebellion).

The app was abandoned.

The company eventually **hired consultants to "fix adoption issues"**—which was **just a fancy way of saying, "Beg people to use the app."**

Lesson Learned:

If employees are **too busy for change**, they'll reject it. **Digital adoption should feel like a relief, not another chore.**

---

4. The Cheat Code for Cultural Change: Make It Personal

People don't resist **change**. They resist **change that feels irrelevant to them**.

Think about it: Nobody complains when **Netflix changes its UI** or **iPhones get new updates**—because those changes make **our lives easier**.

The same applies in business. **When people see how digital transformation benefits them personally, they adopt it faster.**

Example: The Pharma CEO Who Became a "Super User"

One **pharmaceutical CEO** personally started using their company's **new data analytics dashboard** and **publicly shared** how it was helping him make better decisions.

When employees saw the **boss using it daily**, they thought, *"Okay, if even he's using it, I guess we should too."*

Within a year, **adoption rates hit 90%**—not because of force, but because of **influence**.

5. Gamify the Change – Because Humans Love a Challenge

Let's be honest: Most corporate training programs are **as exciting as watching paint dry**.

But what if learning a new system was… fun?

Example: The FMCG "Leaderboard Experiment"

An FMCG company rolled out a new **supply chain analytics tool**. Instead of **forcing** employees to use it, they turned it into a **competition**:

- **Top users were featured on the company's internal leaderboard.**
- **Monthly prizes were given to the most active adopters.**
- **Managers received bonuses based on their team's adoption rates.**

Result? Within **three months**, the system had a **97% adoption rate**.

Why? Because people love winning.

---

6. The "Small Wins" Strategy – One Step at a Time

No one runs a marathon on day one. **Building a digital culture happens in phases.**

Example: The Pharma "One Feature at a Time" Rollout

A **pharmaceutical company** introduced a **complex new research system**. Instead of launching everything at once, they **phased it in**:

- **Month 1:** Only **one key feature** was introduced.
- **Month 2:** A second feature was rolled out, with real-time feedback.
- **Month 3:** Employees started requesting **more features** because they saw the value.

Within six months, what started as **resistance** turned into **demand for more improvements**.

---

7. Celebrate Success – Even the Small Ones

Corporate change is often like **a terrible diet plan**—no one celebrates small wins, so people give up.

Example: The FMCG CEO's Public Thank You

An FMCG company's **CEO publicly thanked** employees who embraced digital change, even for **tiny milestones**.

- **"Shoutout to Anna for saving us 30 minutes a day with the new tool!"**
- **"Mark just closed our first deal using the new CRM—congrats!"**

The result? Employees **wanted to be recognized**, so adoption spread **faster than free coffee on a Monday morning**.

Conclusion: Change Should Feel Like a Gift, Not a Chore

The secret to building a **change-ready culture** isn't **forcing** people to use new systems. It's about making them **want** to.

- **Make it personal**
- **Gamify the experience**
- **Break it into small wins**
- **Celebrate every success**

Because at the end of the day, **people don't resist change—they resist change that feels painful, pointless, or forced.**

So, if you want your company to **actually embrace digital transformation**, don't just **give them a gym membership**.

Make them **fall in love with working out.**

Chapter 11: The Roadmap to Digital Success – From "Good Intentions" to "Real Results"

Introduction: The IKEA Furniture Problem

Ever bought a piece of IKEA furniture?

It starts with **optimism**—you've got all the pieces, a vague idea of how it should look, and the belief that it'll take "just 30 minutes." Fast forward **three hours**, and you're staring at a half-assembled bookshelf, holding **three extra screws** that *must* have come from *somewhere*.

Digital transformation is the IKEA of corporate strategies.

- Leaders **expect quick results**, but reality is a confusing mess of tools, people, and unexpected problems.
- Teams **want to follow the manual**, but halfway through, they realize **the instructions are missing key steps**.
- The final product **kind of works**, but **wobbles** every time someone leans on it.

So, how do you ensure **your digital transformation doesn't end up as an unstable bookshelf**?

Welcome to **The Roadmap to Digital Success**—a step-by-step guide, sprinkled with real-world failures (because let's face it, failure is always funnier) and practical lessons.

Step 1: Start With "Why"—And Make It Personal

Case Study: The FMCG Loyalty Program Nobody Used

A major **FMCG company** launched a **digital customer loyalty program**, investing **millions** in a sleek app. Their logic? "Customers love discounts, so they'll use it!"

Reality?

- Customers **didn't see the value**—they were happy using paper coupons.
- Employees **weren't trained**, so they couldn't explain it properly.
- The **marketing team spoke in corporate jargon**, confusing everyone.

End result? The app had **fewer downloads than a 2010s Nokia ringtone**.

Lesson Learned:

People don't adopt technology **because it's available**—they adopt it when it **solves a problem they actually care about**.

Before launching any digital initiative, ask: **Why should employees and customers care?**

Step 2: Find Your Change Champions (AKA The Digital Cheerleaders)

Case Study: Pharma's Accidental Digital Ambassadors

A pharmaceutical company rolled out a **new AI-powered research tool**. Instead of **forcing** scientists to use it, they identified **early adopters**—the **tech-savvy researchers** who were excited about digital tools.

- These "change champions" **showed their colleagues how it made their lives easier**.
- The adoption rate **tripled** because employees **trusted their peers more than management**.
- Within six months, employees **started requesting MORE digital tools** instead of resisting them.

Lesson Learned:

Peer influence beats corporate mandates. Find your **enthusiastic early adopters**, empower them, and let the transformation spread organically.

Step 3: Keep It Simple—The Fewer Clicks, The Better

Case Study: The FMCG Sales Team's Great Rebellion

A **fast-moving consumer goods (FMCG) giant** rolled out a **new sales CRM system**, claiming it would "revolutionize" how sales teams managed clients.

One small issue…

- The old system required **3 clicks to log a sale**.
- The new system? **15 clicks and a mandatory customer feedback form.**
- Sales reps **hated it** and found a workaround—by **emailing their managers the data**, making the CRM redundant.

Management **couldn't understand why adoption was low**… until an intern pointed out, *"It's just too damn complicated."*

Lesson Learned:

People aren't lazy—they're just **efficient**. If a system takes **more effort than the old way**, people will **find ways around it**.

Before launching a new tool, test it with employees: If they hate it, fix it BEFORE rollout.

Step 4: Make Learning Fun (Or at Least Less Painful)

Case Study: The Pharma Company That Turned Training Into a Netflix Show

A **pharmaceutical firm** introduced a **new compliance tool**, but employees were **dreading the training sessions**. Instead of **boring PowerPoints**, they tried something different:

- They **created short, funny training videos**—starring actual employees, with inside jokes.
- They **gamified training**—offering small rewards for quiz completion.
- They made training **on-demand**, so employees could **learn at their own pace**.

Result?

- **95% completion rate** (compared to the usual 40%).
- Employees **actually understood the system** instead of pretending to.
- People **requested more videos** instead of dreading training.

Lesson Learned:

Training should be **engaging, short, and tailored to real people**—not just a box to check.

Step 5: Track Progress—But Don't Be a Digital Dictator

Case Study: The FMCG Company That Measured the Wrong Metrics

An FMCG company introduced a **new warehouse automation system** and **tracked adoption using login frequency**.

- Employees quickly **figured out the trick**: Log in, click around, **then go back to manual processes**.
- Management saw **high usage numbers**, but productivity **actually dropped**.
- It wasn't until an **anonymous feedback survey** that they realized—employees **weren't using the system properly, they were just gaming the metrics**.

Lesson Learned:

Measure what matters, not vanity metrics. Adoption isn't about how often people log in—it's about **whether they actually use the system to improve their work.**

Step 6: Course-Correct—Because No Plan Survives Reality

Case Study: The Pharma Company That Admitted "We Screwed Up"

A pharmaceutical company **forced** its employees to switch to a **new digital reporting system overnight**.

Within weeks, productivity **plummeted**, and employees were **furious**.

Instead of **doubling down**, leadership did something shocking: **They admitted their mistake.**

- They held **town hall meetings** to hear employee frustrations.
- They **paused the rollout** and **made key improvements** based on real feedback.
- They **relaunched it in phases**, with better training and support.

End result? Employees **actually appreciated the company's transparency** and engaged with the revised system.

Lesson Learned:

A digital roadmap should be **flexible**. If something isn't working, **fix it, don't force it.**

Step 7: Celebrate Wins—Even the Small Ones

Ever noticed how companies celebrate big milestones, but never small ones? That's like **only cheering for Olympic gold medalists** but ignoring everyone who just finished their first 5K.

Example: The FMCG Company That Rewarded "Digital Firsts"

Instead of waiting for **100% digital transformation**, an FMCG company **celebrated small wins**:

- First employee to successfully use the new system got a **public shoutout.**
- First team to complete 100% digital reporting got a **pizza party.**
- Teams that consistently adopted the new process got **bonus points in performance reviews.**

End result? Employees actually **wanted to be part of the digital transformation**—not because they had to, but because **it was rewarding**.

Conclusion: Digital Transformation is a Marathon, Not a Sprint

The **difference between digital success and digital failure** isn't technology—it's **people.**

- **Start with WHY** – Make it personal.
- **Find your digital cheerleaders** – Peer influence beats corporate mandates.
- **Make adoption EASY** – The fewer clicks, the better.
- **Gamify and celebrate** – Fun beats force, always.
- **Be flexible** – Admit mistakes, course-correct, and keep improving.

Because at the end of the day, **a roadmap isn't about the destination—it's about making sure everyone enjoys the journey.**

So, are you **forcing digital change**, or are you **leading a movement**?

Because if you do it right, people won't just **follow your roadmap**—they'll **help build the highway.**

Conclusion: From Resistance to Resilience – Making Digital Transformation Work for People

---

The $1 Million Question: Why Does Digital Transformation Fail?

If you've made it this far, you already know the **biggest secret** about digital transformation:

Technology isn't the problem. People are.

But not in the way most leaders think.

People don't resist **technology**—they resist **poorly executed change**. They resist **being forced into systems that make their jobs harder**, **not knowing why a change is happening**, and **feeling left out of decisions that impact them**.

That's why so many **well-intentioned digital transformations fail spectacularly**.

The Digital Transformation Graveyard: Why Good Intentions Aren't Enough

Think back to some of the real-world horror stories we covered in this book:

- **The FMCG company that spent millions on an AI system**—only for employees to reject it because it was too complicated.
- **The construction firm that introduced digital blueprints**—but site engineers ignored them because the old way felt more "real."
- **The pharmaceutical company that launched a compliance tool**—but employees found workarounds because no one trained them properly.

What do all these failures have in common?

They weren't **technology problems**.

They were **people problems** caused by **bad leadership, poor communication, lack of training, and a failure to understand human behavior**.

The Success Blueprint: What the Best Companies Get Right

But there were also stories of **digital success**—companies that cracked the code and made transformation **work for their people, not against them**.

What did they do differently?

- **They started with "why"** – They made the change personal and meaningful.
- **They found digital champions** – They let early adopters lead the way.
- **They simplified everything** – The fewer clicks, the better.
- **They gamified and celebrated progress** – Because fun beats force.
- **They admitted mistakes and adapted** – Instead of forcing broken systems.

These companies understood that **transformation is a process, not an event**.

It's not about launching technology. It's about embedding it into culture.

The Road Ahead: How You Can Lead the Change

By now, you might be wondering:

"How do I make sure my organization doesn't end up in the digital graveyard?"

Here's your **action plan**:

1. **Change your mindset** – Stop thinking of digital transformation as an "IT project." It's a **human transformation project.**
2. **Listen to employees** – Involve them **before** decisions are made, not after.
3. **Make adoption easy** – If a system takes more effort than the old way, it's already doomed.
4. **Measure what matters** – Track **real usage and impact**, not vanity metrics.
5. **Celebrate the journey** – Recognize small wins, make training engaging, and keep morale high.

Because at the end of the day, **digital transformation isn't about technology**.

It's about **people.**

And when you put **people first**, technology follows.

Final Thought: Are You a Dictator or a Digital Leader?

Many leaders **push** digital change onto their employees. But the best ones **pull** people toward it.

So, ask yourself:

- **Are you a digital dictator?** – Forcing systems, ignoring resistance, and blaming employees when adoption fails?
- **Or are you a digital leader?** – Inspiring change, making adoption easy, and creating a culture where transformation happens naturally?

Because if you do it right, you won't have to **force** digital transformation.

Your people will **want** it.

And that's when true transformation begins.